A LIFE COMPASS FOR SUCCESS

THE STORY OF A WOMAN'S COURAGE AND
OUTREACH TO TROUBLED YOUTHS ON
HER ENTREPRENEURSHIP JOURNEY

HENNY GOH

Copyright © 2017 by Henny Goh Hwee Hoon

ISBN - 13 : 978-1975973667
ISBN - 10 : 197-5973666

All rights reserved. No part of this publication may be reproduced, stored in a retrieval system, or transmitted in any form or by any means, electronic, mechanical, photocopying, recording or otherwise, without the prior permission of the copyright owner.

ACKNOWLEDGEMENT

I'd like to express my love and gratitude to my late parents who had brought me to this world and taught me the value of life. I'd also like to thank my family for supporting me in life and inspiring me to write this book. I have a great husband who allows me creative license and three gorgeous children who are my greatest pillars of strength in life.

This book marks my debut as an author and I have many friends to thank who have contributed in one way or another towards the creation of this book. My deep appreciation to all of you for your kind support.

FOREWORD

This book from Henny "A Life Compass For Success", is undoubtedly a great labor of love. It resonates deeply with my own philosophies on life. Not only is it inspiring but practical as well, with so many great role models and compelling examples. Henny's advice is both inspiring and practical, with many gems to take away. The journey to be 'the master of our fate and the captain of our soul' translates directly into living a life of purpose, meaning and fulfillment. Henny shows us that part of the life journey is about uncovering the 'nuggets of gold' that we all have in us - our talents, passion and aspirations - and to use every twist and turn in life as an opportunity to discover more of these nuggets out of which we can learn and grow. This journey in self-mastery and self-realization is guided by a Life Compass, the central theme of this book.

I cannot overstate the importance of a Life Compass - my own life journey has been transformed by having a personal mission statement that acted as my Life Compass for over 30 years. It guided the course of my life and help lead to where I am today, where I have found joy and fulfillment despite great setbacks. In sharing her life journey as an entrepreneur and mentor to troubled youths - changing the course of their life by asking them to listen to their own inner voice, following their heart, giving them hope and the permission to dream, the author has demonstrated the essence of happiness - that happiness is within us, and that the best way to make ourselves happy is to make others happy. It gives life meaning – manifesting compassion with wisdom in the service of others is the highest form of human fulfillment. This is her legacy.

I'd also like to take this opportunity to share with you excerpts from Chapter 7 of the book "The Success DNA of Extraordinary Entrepreneurs", by best-selling author Selina Seah, where I talked about the 5 'P's and the 5 'C's a lot. I did not come up with the 5 'P's – it is referred to quite often. The 5 'P's are: 1) Passion, 2) People, 3) Profits, 4) Perseverance, 5) Pivot.

Passion is important to propel what you do, you certainly need perseverance to keep going because there will be lots of obstacles along the way. You would need to be able to work with people – no successful entrepreneurs can build an enterprise on their own, they need a team around them who can complement their talents. Profits are obvious for sustainability, and finally you need the agility and flexibility to pivot. Pivot means being able to change directions if needed. The 5 'C's are what I look for personally. They are: 1) Compassion, 2) Courage, 3) Curiosity, 4) Commitment, 5) Calm.

Compassion helps you feel others' pain and see their suffering, and in wanting to help alleviate that pain, that suffering. Compassion and love is the most powerful force in the universe, the source of all creative energy, and creative power.

Courage to be different and to take the path less travelled, courage to embrace change, courage to be the change. The 'Gandhis' of the world, the change makers all have great courage in them.

Curiosity is the appetite for learning new things, acquiring new knowledge, and seeking new experiences. It's staying hungry and staying foolish.

Commitment is something that's somewhat lacking these days, which is the conviction to do and achieve great things. We need commitment despite uncertainties. Of course we need to do our homework, but at times you just have to commit, and then surprisingly the resources will come to you.

Commitment is not what your mind thinks, commitment is your intuition, how you feel, and to follow that with concrete action. Commitment to a cause or purpose is the foundation to a meaningful life.

Calm is a state of mind. A healthy mind is a calm mind, a clear mind. Great things can only be accomplished with a calm and clear mind. Creativity can only come from a calm mind.

We also need to develop more intuition, especially for entrepreneurs, for any endeavor really. We all think too much and feel too little. When I was younger, working as an engineer and scientist and loving mathematics, it was all left brain activities. Today however, I do things mostly based on intuition. I don't think or try to rationalize too much, mostly I just feel. It's something I think anyone can develop. It's about quieting your rational mind, allowing your intuitive mind, your higher self to come to the fore. Follow your heart and your intuition.

When I first started my business in 1997, it was all based on intuition. I was still in Apple and I had other opportunities waiting for me, but my intuition told me to do it, and it turned out to be right.

There is a saying, "When you come to a crossroad, always take the path less travelled." When you take the path less travelled, new opportunities and new vistas always emerge. I have always taken this approach to life; people sometimes think I'm crazy, but for me, it's taking the path less travelled. This approach has really served me well; it allowed me to learn new things, create new opportunities and take on new challenges. So have the courage to take a path less travelled – and perhaps more importantly, to be there at the crossroads.

There are so many similarities in our philosophies and approach to life. I wish you every success in the launch of this new book.

Sincerely,

Yen-Lu Chow

Co-founder & President, Whole Tree Foundation / Over-The-Rainbow, Co-founder & Chairman, Singapore Creations Etc, Executive Director, BAF Spectrum, and Founding Partner, Fatfish Medialab.

BOOK REVIEWS AND TESTIMONIALS

"A very thoughtful and well written piece... ensures that the reader turns the page to find out what is next... everybody needs a Life Compass!"

Dr Shahul Hameed
Dental Surgeon
Senior Lecturer (Adjunct)
Faculty of Dentistry, National University of Singapore

"I like to share a quote from Pike's Fourth Law "Learning has not taken place until behavior has changed". In life many want to improve but very few want to change.

Henny had put up a very easy to read and simple to understand book with her real life knowledge and sharing her wealth of experience. A learned good wife and mother of three, a successful entrepreneur, a committed Rotarian and a selfless pro bono social worker to the community.

The book "A Life Compass For Success" is a blue print for success towards your goals and what you like to be. Her Life Compass of NSEW is not controlled by the universe but it is you to make a change if you had not done so.

Her sharing of her experience, encounters and guidance will benefit the young and the seniors too. Her take on positive thinking and adaptability to make the appropriate changes in your choice of destiny is inspiring.

Just remember that what you are today will be what you become tomorrow."

Johnson Tan
Managing Director
Tantex Pte Ltd

"Profound. The Life Compass Nature (North), Environment (East), Self (South), Wealth (West) has never been shared before. It creates a sense of purpose, direction and action. We should share these with the youths in our Rotary district and beyond.

All the best and I hope you will share your book with more people. "

Philip Chong Mau Kiong
Rotary Club of Likas Bay
Past District Governor 2015-2016
Rotary District 3310

"Before I knew about the Life Compass, I was a very energetic teen with a lot of ambition and pride but very little wisdom, and even lesser knowledge on how to do or what to say. I always wanted to do great things but I was very unsure and was constantly procrastinating on doing things.

However, once I learned about the Life Compass, I was able to set my life straight and slowly take baby steps forward in my life to make small achievements and do small things with great love. Becoming the Rotaract District Representative is one of my biggest achievements, and I would like to give credit to Rotarian Henny and her incredible Life Compass in helping me move forward in life and become a successful leader.

There are many obstacles as a youth, and having good leaders such as Henny who empowers youths to go forward and far in life, will make the future a much easier and manageable path. I would like to say thank you, for being a great motivator and a great mentor."

Rytha Lew Chiu Min
District Rotaract Representative RY 2017/2018
Rotaract Club of Raffles City
District 3310, Zone 3, Singapore

"What a great book you wrote. In short I will say, Dream Big, Start small, Be focused and DO IT NOW. Take the first step towards the dream."

Capt Budi Soehardi
CNN Hero, Retired Pilot, Full Time Father with Roslin Orphanage, Indonesia

"The invaluable advice in this book can only be given by someone who has long thought about youths and their problems, and has long experience helping them. The book is truly a compass for young people who feel lost and have difficulty coping with life."

Soh Gim Chuan
Partner at Soh Wong & Yap
Solicitor, Author, Tutor, Trainer

"In general, it is a useful book for the youths and people who are still struggling in life and work. A good life guide for many people."

Wilma Wen
Managing Director
CA Indosuez Wealth Management, Hong Kong

"Congratulations to Henny Goh on the publication of her book "A Life Compass for Success".

I have known Henny for about forty years. She is helpful, tolerant and a person of integrity. She plays her roles well as a wife, a mother and a volunteer worker. She is a good and passionate mentor to misled youths who have lost their directions in life.

I am sure this book will motivate more youths to seek the right direction in life and march towards a brighter future with courage and determination.

I hope the author's endeavor will encourage each youngster to reach out and achieve their own personal goals in life."

Lee Kim Foong
Retired Teacher

"Henny's book offers a very realistic and practical perspective in acquiring a meaningful and successful life. A very simple concept of the Life Compass, it provides a simple direction to embark on the road to success. This book contain objectives and programs that are certainly relevant and useful in guiding youths to acquire success in life."

Henry K H Tan
Group Managing Director
Alpha-Health (Asia) Pte Ltd
President
Association of Medical Device Industry (Singapore)

"In a digital age where we are bombarded with lots of information, the Life Compass offers a simplistic yet effective approach followed by many successful people. Instead of trying 101 things that might work, the author is focusing on the key points that have helped many successful entrepreneurs and business people, and put the reasons and mindset they had for their success in this book. It is not only telling their story but also asking you the questions to reflect where you are, where you want to be and act as a compass to reach your destination. You may have heard many of the advice listed over here and even much more. However, this book is getting rid of all the fluff and many other hard to apply techniques and focusing on a plentiful list of the pointers that are the core to have inner peace, understanding yourself and eliminate procrastination to be happy, successful and achieve your dreams in life."

Ozan Turay
Website Optimization Expert
Getbuzz.net

"Henny brings with her many years of wisdom and as a counselor, she has helped many find their own vista. This is a book about coping with uncertainty and the stress of dealing with our future surrounded by ambiguity. It is a book that encourages own self reflection to find your own purpose and passion in life. Henny aptly include many simple truths and life tools that we have long forgotten in her book. These are powerful tools that fire your imagination on who you are and what you live for. I encourage all to read this book and I believe it will inspire you to choose a life path that is uniquely yours that brings fulfillment and happiness to yourself, your family and friends around you."

Tay Woon Teck
Managing Director, Risk Advisory
RSM Risk Advisory Pte Ltd

ABOUT THE AUTHOR

Henny Goh was born into a traditional Chinese family and her six years in a Chinese primary school instilled in her a love for Chinese literature and poems. She enjoys travelling and writing and expanding her vista by learning new things.

Henny started her business at the age of 25 fulfilling her dream of being a business woman. She travelled extensively to Europe, India, China, Korea and many other countries for her business ventures and launched many new products in the local and overseas markets. All this while she nurtured a childhood dream of becoming a teacher. She is actively involved in volunteering work especially with youths and delivered pro bono extracurricular classes on Entrepreneurship and talks on her Life Compass to schools and colleges. She has organized many youth programs for Rotary in both Malaysia and Singapore.

She joined Rotary in 1995 and had served in the Foundation of Rotary Clubs of Singapore, Rotary Family Center, Ayer-Raja Student Care Center and Rotary Counseling Center. She is also an active member of The Society of Modern Management Singapore and CEO Reading Club, and a Committee Member of Modern Confucianism Foundation since 2014.

She has eventually realized her wish to conceptualize The Life Compass in the form of a book after spending many years of research and searching for an answer to help those who are in need of a direction in life. "A Life Compass For Success" marks Henny Goh's debut as an author.

CONTENTS

	Acknowledgement	V
	Foreword	VI
	Book Reviews and Testimonials	XI
	About The Author	XX
1.	Lost	1
2.	Where Do I Go From Here and Making Resolutions	5
3.	Is the Destination Important or the Journey?	15
4.	You Need a Life Compass	21
5.	Our Environment Matters	27
6.	Achieving Wealth	33
7.	Working with Nature Laws	41
8.	Examining My Self	51
9.	Think Big	57
10.	SOS, EOE, NON, WOW	65

LOST

THE LIFE COMPASS

01
LOST

The teenage boy thought his life was over. He was lost and afraid. Very afraid. It's the time of the year to make New Year resolutions but he did not know where to start. He just drew a blank. He does not have a plan, unlike his peers. He is sixteen, turning seventeen and hasn't earned a penny in his life. His future seems bleak. He studied for a course his parents wanted him to but has not the slightest inclination or passion to pursue a career or vocation in that direction. As it was a course of study he is not interested in, he fared badly and graduated at the bottom of the class. Needless to say, he got a shelling from his parents. Wallowing in self-pity and misery, New Year's Eve was probably one of the worst nights he had to live through. While others made merry and went to party at some countdown party or watch

> *"Write your injuries in dust, your benefits in Marble"*
> *-- Benjamin Franklin*

the fireworks at Marina Bay Sands, he felt so empty inside and an absolute failure. "How can 2017 be better than 2016?", the teenage boy thought. He lacks direction and a compass in his life. He does not know where he is heading. He does not know what his future holds.

Does this sound like a familiar tale? I have encountered this many a time in my volunteer work with youths. Many youths like Eryan do not have a plan for most things in their lives. They simply coasted along. They also do not have a voice if they have parents who are control freaks or live their lives through their children.

Then one day the teenager spotted a motivational poster. It looked like this. Hmmn, 'vista'. Big word. What does this mean? The teenager whipped out his smart phone and did a Google search for the word meaning.

According to the Merriam-Webster LearnersDictionary.com, the word 'vista' means a large number of things that may be possible in the future. He felt a stirring in his heart. He felt hopeful. He now feels there is an ocean of possibilities in his life. But where does he start?

WHERE DO I GO FROM HERE AND MAKING RESOLUTIONS

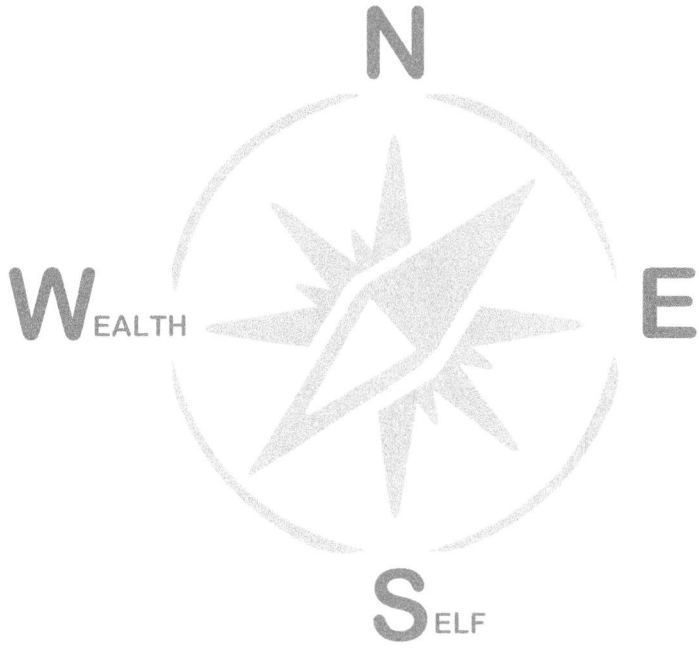

THE LIFE COMPASS

02

WHERE DO I GO FROM HERE AND MAKING RESOLUTIONS

A voice inside Eryan told him, "Take baby steps." And then the voice whispered, "If you really want to be successful, stay away from the naysayers and don't let negative thoughts get in your way. Be positive and act on your dreams. Just do it!"

Many people fail because they give up even before they succeed. Or they simply do not know where to start. Or they talk themselves out of it before they take action for their dreams. You will never achieve your dreams unless you know exactly what you want; where you want to go; are passionate about your goal, and have a plan of action.

"Ambition is the path to success. Persistence is the vehicle you arrive in."
*-- **Bill Bradley***

In my frequent talks to youth leadership groups and school students, I was deeply inspired listening to the dreams of the teenagers. These youths felt it was ok to dream and be proud of your achievements and where you want to go in life. As a speaker and leadership mentor in my pro bono trainings, I help people to discover their passion and empower them to achieve their dreams in life. I often ask, "Where do you see yourself three to five years from now? " The teenagers that I spoke to at my last presentation have dreams for their life and where they see themselves in the future. But not Eryan. Eryan was retiring and shy, and turned up for class late with unkempt hair. The son of an accountant and a lawyer, the picture of him ending up like his parents in the future is extremely frightening to him! He hates numbers and lawyers, and wish they would burn in hell. I did not scold Eryan for being late. Instead I spoke to the youths about how important it is to have a buddy, who will push you on, motivate you and let you know how awesome it is to have a dream. As their leadership mentor, my job is to guide them towards achieving their dream.

I wrote on the white board and asked the teenagers to ask themselves these life-changing questions:

1) What is your passion?

2) Who is your buddy?

3) What is your dream in life?

4) Where do you see yourself going three to five years from now?

I told them to spend some time reflecting on the questions that weekend, and that I'd check in with them at the next session.

Leaders set goals. You should break your goals down into small action steps. Set short-term, mid-term and long-term goals. Franklin D. Roosevelt overcame a personal tragedy of polio which cost him the use of his legs to become the 32nd President of the United States at age 51, in the midst of its worst economic crisis. He served in the White House office for 12 years until his death on April 12, 1945. President Roosevelt brought about remarkable reform and relief for the unemployed and farmers, and great economic growth for the country. The oldest US President to be inaugurated is currently Donald Trump who assumed office this year at age 70. What matters is not your age, but if you have a dream, and whether you are willing to pay the price for it by taking action. Actually taking action is the most difficult step for many people.

Dr. Stephen William Hawking was diagnosed with motor neurone disease at the age of 21 which left him paralyzed. He was only given two years to live. Professor Hawking,

> *"Ambition is the path to success. Persistence is the vehicle you arrive in."*
> *-- **Bill Bradley***

now 75, was a Professor of Mathematics at Cambridge from 1979 until 2009 – the position once held by Sir Isaac Newton. He married twice, and has three children. He went on to become one of the greatest theoretical physicists that the world has ever known when he is supposed to have died at 23. Professor Hawking has twelve honorary degrees. He is still an active part of Cambridge University and retains an office at the Department for Applied Maths and Theoretical Physics. His title is now the Dennis Stanton Avery and Sally Tsui Wong-Avery Director of Research at the Department of Applied Mathematics and Theoretical Physics. In spite of being wheelchair bound and dependent on a computerized voice system for communication by a single cheek muscle, Professor Hawking did not allow his disability to stop him from being a useful citizen of the world, a bestselling author and a renowned theoretical physicist. He has not stopped dreaming and still hopes to make it into space one day. This is a remarkable man who believes in the power of his dreams.

So it is not important how old you are, or what circumstances you were born into. What matters is you must heed your own inner voice, see your vista in your mind, and have a dream. And of course, act on it.

> *"The people who are crazy enough to think they can change the world are the ones who do."*
> **—Apple's "Think Different" commercial, 1997**

Did you know that the iconic American co-founder of Apple Inc., Steve Jobs, in the past lacking direction, dropped out of college after six months? Jobs was bright and in his youth, frustrated over formal schooling. He was bored in elementary school and played pranks, and his fourth-grade teacher had to bribe him to study. Jobs did so well in tests that administrators wanted to skip him ahead to high school—a proposal that his adopted parents declined. When he was at high school, he met his future partner Steve Wozniak. In 1976, when Jobs was just 21, he and Wozniak started Apple Computer in the Jobs family garage, funding their entrepreneurial dream by Jobs selling his Volkswagen bus and Wozniak selling his beloved scientific calculator. Steve Jobs was ousted from the company he founded in 1985, returned to rescue it from near bankruptcy in 1997, and by the time he died from cancer in October 2011, had built it into the world's most valuable company. Steve Jobs will long be remembered for giving us the iPhone and how he applied imagination to technology and business. He left the world a legacy and great management lessons.

Few people have the courage to act on their dreams. They keep giving excuses and procrastination kills their dreams. They say things like, "I'm not rich enough", "I'm not educated enough", "I'm not handsome or pretty", "I'm not gifted", "It's past my time", "You can't teach an old dog new tricks".

"Ambition is the path to success. Persistence is the vehicle you arrive in."
*-- **Bill Bradley***

Procrastination is knowing what you must do, and yet you don't do it. There's always tomorrow. Although procrastination is illogical, it actually reveals your unconscious fears and your self-imposed limitations and beliefs. The major cause is fear, your fear of taking action. At some unconscious level, your mind searches for a reason that links the action to a painful experience. So your unconscious mind will 'protect' you as it associates pain to the action. We are wired to reach for pleasure, not pain so you procrastinate on the tasks that do not feel good at the moment.

Eliminate excuses. And perhaps you will have to consider eliminating people from your life who keep you away from making your dreams come true. Apart from making New Year resolutions and sticking with it, it's time to do some spring-cleaning in your circle of friends and on social media. We all come to a point in our lives, when we need to re-evaluate our relationships.

You may also need to re-evaluate your resolutions. Take a step back and examine each one. Are they resolutions you wanted to make or resolutions others have told you to make? Is this a resolution something you definitely want to keep? Or a half-hearted attempt at reaching a goal that you really aren't interested in reaching. If your resolution needs to be modified, do it now. Resolutions, like goals, are for your benefit, not your detriment. Your attitude toward a particular resolution will help you determine whether you want to keep it or not. Any resolution made which doesn't have your enthusiasm backing it will be forgotten altogether by the end of the year. Make resolutions that matter and that you can keep.

Here are 6 tips that will increase your chances of achieving your New Year Resolutions:

1. Simplify your life.
2. Give up toxic relationships or people in your life.
3. Plan for growth, no matter how insignificant or small.
4. Challenge yourself.
5. Stick with your goals every day.
6. Take action.

"Ambition is the path to success. Persistence is the vehicle you arrive in."
*-- **Bill Bradley***

IS THE DESTINATION IMPORTANT OR THE JOURNEY?

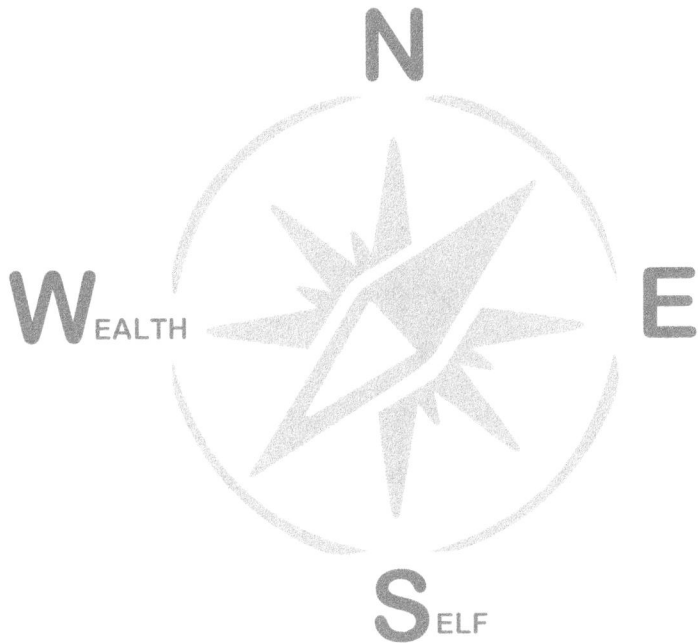

THE LIFE COMPASS

03

IS THE DESTINATION IMPORTANT OR THE JOURNEY?

Many people think that success is a destination. To me, success is a journey, just like life. It is a continuous journey to learn and grow. We all aspire to have success in life. We talk about it, read up on it, envy those who achieve it, trade our health for it, lose sleep over it and struggle to achieve it. Success comes in many forms, usually with attaining our goals. Success brings great satisfaction and happiness. It gives us a reason to be happy every day. Sadly, society equates success with the attainment of

> *"We must free ourselves of the hope that the sea will ever rest. We must learn to sail in high winds."* -- **Aristotle Onassis**

wealth. There is nothing wrong with this worldview but often happiness is an end product of success. Money cannot buy happiness.

Success is less about money than it is about value creation. If you look at what you've contributed to society and are satisfied with what you see, you are also a successful person. If you're happy, you've succeeded. If we commit to achieve small goals every day, step by step we will be approaching our dream sooner than we expect. That's what I also shared with the youths at my next volunteer session. I saw a spark in Eryan's eyes and I knew my words meant something to him. His face lit up when I further elaborated on the topic of Happiness with the group.

The secret to real happiness is neither to be rich nor to accumulate money for the future to live lavishly. It's much more important that you identify what it is that you like to do with your life and your passion. And once you find it, see how you can incorporate it into your life. Since we spend a great part of our lives sleeping or at work, you might as well be working at a job that you love. Then you'll be on the road to happiness. That's success. I was getting better at counseling; I was guiding my charges towards what they want to do and making positive changes that will make them happier with my Life Compass. I got a lot of satisfaction doing what I love and watching the youths blossom under my care.

I worked with Eryan as his mentor in a few sessions. He was not sure what it is he wants to do in life and have no dreams for the future. In fact, it drew a scary blank. First I had to deal with his anger and his issue with authority. His parents controlled every aspect of his life and didn't care what he wanted. I told him he could not change his parents but he could change the man in the mirror. I told him, "You have to start dreaming again." I told him to write down his goals and to make a list. Picture his goals clearly in his mind. Find images of what he would like to own. Get into details. Then imagine himself already achieving those goals three to five years from now. I told him to shoot for the stars; it doesn't matter if he lands halfway. What matters is that he has tried. At the end of my third closed door session with Eryan, he reached out to give me a hug with tears in his eyes. I was his first mentor, and the first person who showed him love and care. I felt a deep satisfaction and knew I had succeeded. I went to bed that night very happy. That was a breakthrough in my work with youths. I could work for little or no reward, and still be very successful as this has become my life mission – to make a difference in the world.

"We must free ourselves of the hope that the sea will ever rest. We must learn to sail in high winds." -- **Aristotle Onassis**

What occupies your time and your thoughts? Do you know people who are caught up with the action of busy-ness but with no clear vision and purpose? Their hands are busy, they have no time for this or that but their destination is unclear! Even when they take action, they show they're not fully aware of where they're going. Since they're not really sure of where they're going, they may settle for something less than what they started at the outset. Don't settle for second best! Know what goals are worthy to pursue. Then pursue your goals relentlessly and see yourself achieving the goals by a set timeline. But enjoy the journey and the landscape as you go after your dreams.

Do not show worry the door and invite fear into your life. Know that it will work this time. Fear has no place in our life. Life is about highs and lows and we are going to have problems anyway. We just need to know how to deal with them. Worry and fear is not the way to do it. You have never fixed anything in your life by worrying about it. If it got better, it's not because you worried about it; it's more than likely because you have found a solution and didn't settle for mediocrity. Success is doing what you believe in, taking responsibility for your actions. It also involves goal setting and taking a good honest look at yourself is helpful to determine what you really want in life, what needs changing and where you want to go. You should also be proud of the goals you have already achieved, no matter how small.

YOU NEED A LIFE COMPASS

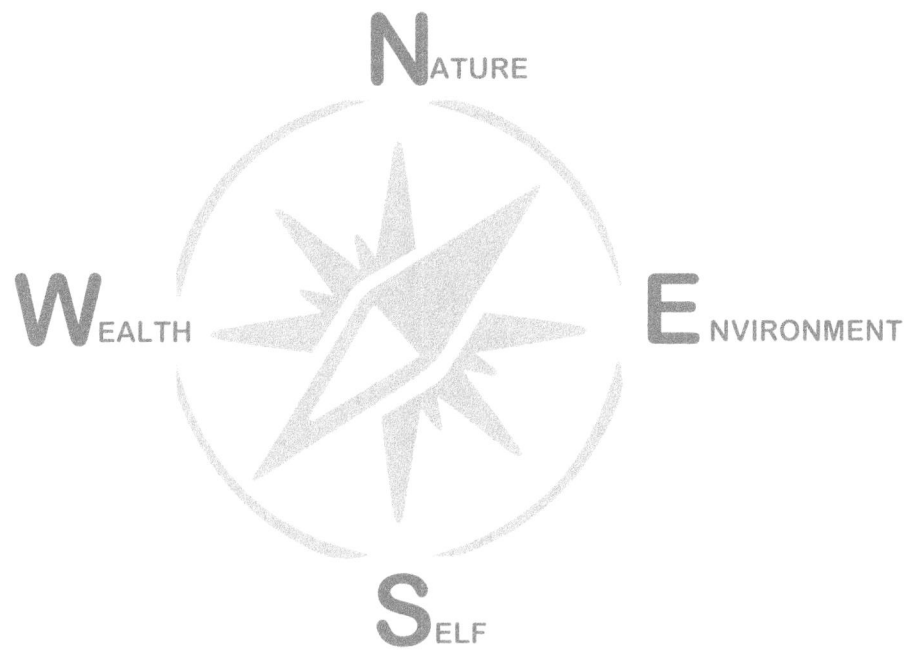

THE LIFE COMPASS

04
YOU NEED A LIFE COMPASS

Many of my students come to me feeling like life is out of control. They felt as though circumstances and people ran their lives and controlled everything that they did. They told me their life sucks. They do not think they are the master of their fate, the captain of their soul. There are many ways that people can feel a loss of control in their lives. We can lose control through failure, retrenchment, debt, a death in the family, a life-threatening illness, frustration, burnout, depression, stagnation, change, and trauma. However, one of the most common ways is playing the victim's role and unconsciously giving away your power to others.

> *"I am the master of my fate. I am the captain of my soul."*
> *– **William Henley***

In my counseling sessions, I worked with these clients to list some specific situations in which they felt this way and how they felt out of control in the situation. We talked about how when growing up, parental voices controlled us and asked us to live by their rules. It's interesting to note that for some clients, the sight of authority figures like teachers and bosses can trigger a reflex action to seek "parental acceptance" and they felt an overwhelming sense of self-doubt and guilt creeping into their world. These are the clear signs that they have relinquished control. This is an unconscious act, and you can begin to live by the rules and dictates of the other person. External stimuli and people can trigger that basic childhood instinct of seeking parental acceptance for things that you do simply by making you doubt yourself. You then surrender your own belief systems and adopt those of the other party. You begin to live in someone else's context. No wonder you feel that your life is out of control. Live your own life by replacing these triggers with your own rules for living. Unless you want to be tied to your mother's apron strings, it's time to break this cycle! Learn to accept yourself and not wait for others, as in the long run you are the only person who has a stake in your own life and in making your own decisions if you want to be successful.

The key to success in life and to feeling fulfilled is to simply listen to your inner self and have a compass that will point you to where you want to go, what you love to do and help you achieve your dreams. A compass will help you to stay on top of your game and acts as a navigation tool guiding you towards your goals, and putting you back in control of your life.

So what is a Life Compass? By my own definition, it is a tool to understand and connect with Nature's laws from above (N), examine our Self (S) and taking action to achieve our Wealth (W) while working with the external influences of our Environment (E). It looks simplistic but it is amazing how often people (including me) sit daydreaming about our goals and staring at a paper with a list of all the steps to be taken and become so depressed by the thought of all the work to be done that we do nothing for days and weeks, even months! It's so easy to talk ourselves out of chasing our dreams. You can choose to stop looking at this piece of paper and do something about it. Or do nothing.

The Jewish Rabbis teach their students to deal with the problem of studying a huge syllabus (the Talmud) by telling the story of the heap of dust. Two men were asked to move a huge heap of dust. One man soon gave up saying: "We'll never move this! It's far too big." The other man kept

> *"I am the master of my fate. I am the captain of my soul."*
> *– **William Henley***

at it day after day moving a little at a time. It seemed like he was achieving nothing but eventually the heap began to look a little smaller. Finally he cleared the whole heap away and received his reward. I have worked with a youth who is often stressed out over studying for an exam and what he has not done. Since his home environment is not conducive for studying, he would take his books to the void deck below his flat, listened to music that he loves with his ear phones, and studied every day for two hours, sometimes three. He did something and made a pain point become a pleasurable event. He wisely decided to take action to put things right. He did not ace his exam but at least he passed it. This young man remembered not to play the victim's role.

To use another example: Your problem could be a debt. So destroy your debt by plugging the little leaks in your finances which are draining your money away. Must you have that Starbucks Grande coffee in the morning? Do you really need that new shirt or dress? It all adds up. I eat my breakfast at home. I shop at bargain stores or for sales items on my travels. It's not because I cannot afford it. I am cultivating the habit of the rich.

Cut down on your expenses and your luxuries, and you'll be amazed by how much money you can put aside for a rainy day. Success is not overnight. Chip away at a problem bit by bit and eventually your problem will disappear. So stop feeling depressed about what you haven't done. Start fixing things bit by bit or pay someone else to do the job for you. You have to save your time and energy for other more important and urgent tasks, such as setting goals and achieving your dreams. Step by step. Rome is not built in a day.

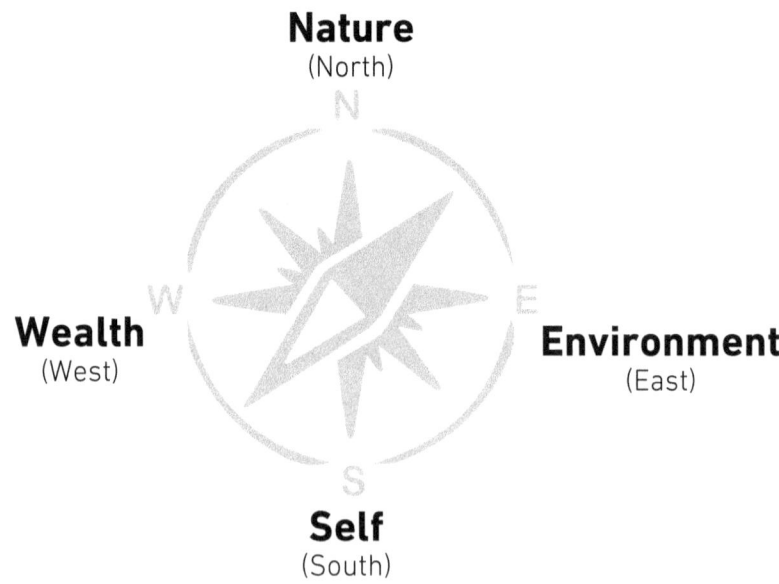

OUR ENVIRONMENT MATTERS

THE LIFE COMPASS

05

OUR ENVIRONMENT MATTERS

I have a friend who always notices the architecture of quaint buildings, shapes and colors. As a child, her childhood dream was to become an artist. Her parents who are not highly educated, discouraged her from pursuing what they felt was not a good way to make a living. They probably have not heard of Picasso and that good paintings by famous artists could sell for thousands and millions of dollars. My friend says with a sad look on her face, that her parents killed her dream in its infancy. She never became an artist, but married one. She became her husband's muse and today she accompanies her husband on art exhibitions.

> *"The only thing you can change is yourself,
> but often it is enough to change everything."* -- **Gary W Goldstein**

Dreams are fragile and we must nurture them. It is important not to talk about them to anyone whom we sense will not support them. I have known since my adult working life that I wanted to teach. No one in my family supported my dream at that time. I also wanted to write on a topic close to my heart. In 2002, as an active Rotarian and a member of the Management Council running our Rotary Family Services Center and Rotary Counseling Center, I was exposed to many realistic problems faced by people from all walks of life including troubled youths. There were a few cases that really broke my heart. A poignant example is a teenage boy who wanted to drop out from school because his parents had just gone through divorce proceedings and his father was living with another woman and could not afford to pay alimony to the family. The family was suddenly broken into pieces. The poor boy had to face a depressed housewife mother with a younger sister to look after. He was totally lost and didn't know what to do, what his future direction is and what his future would look like. I felt very upset for the family and wondered at that point of time if only they had a Life Compass that will help them to find a direction and guide the family out of this dilemma, it could bring some answers and alleviate the pain. I could not understand why so many people must be sentenced to a life of misery and suffer from someone else's mistake.

Subsequently in another Rotary club project "Staying Connected", I visited many old age homes, day care centers and hospices, and those experiences prompted me to inquire a lot more about life. Why are we born to undergo aging, sickness and death which cannot be avoided in life, but brought much misery to the people it afflicted? That was a life-defining moment. From that moment on, I knew that my subconscious mind has been working on gathering information after many years of studying people's behavior and my involvement in volunteer activities with the young and old. I developed this Life Compass tool which I hope can be of help to many people who are in difficulty and need guidance and answers to solve their problems.

For years I managed to write in my diary and secretly worked on my story while running a business. I doodled and wrote many pages of notes and put them away in my drawer. I would often look at my diagrams and handwritten notes and wonder when it would see the light of day as a physical book. I've worked on writing this book for over five years and juggled my role as a wife with bringing up my children and managing a business before I found the courage to publish it.

"The only thing you can change is yourself, but often it is enough to change everything." -- **Gary W Goldstein**

Many gurus in self-development stress the importance of getting support for your dream. This support can come from teachers, mentors, coaches, role models and colleagues. Friends can also lend their support, when they don't belittle your dream and project their fears and doubts on you. Your support group can make a difference and you can soar like the eagles.

A key valuable ingredient to be a successful person is to be genuinely interested in helping others, and show your interest in them. How well you relate to others and their needs will help you expand your network of friends and social circle, and develop bonds that last.

I have this former colleague in my office from the United Kingdom who wanted to learn Mandarin. As I am fluent in speaking and writing in Chinese, I decided to reach out to him. We spent our lunch breaks together and met after work to swap stories about food, culture, people, and places of interest. After a couple of years, he could speak fairly good conversational Mandarin and we became good friends. He now has an opportunity to speak Mandarin in his workplace and my command of English has also improved after practicing it with a native speaker!

Just by showing sincerity and taking the time to understand another person's culture, behavior, language, and a different viewpoint, you can plant good seeds for success and learn the art of influence. This shouldn't be for personal gain or selfish reasons. It is best when your intention is for the common good of a group.

ACHIEVING WEALTH

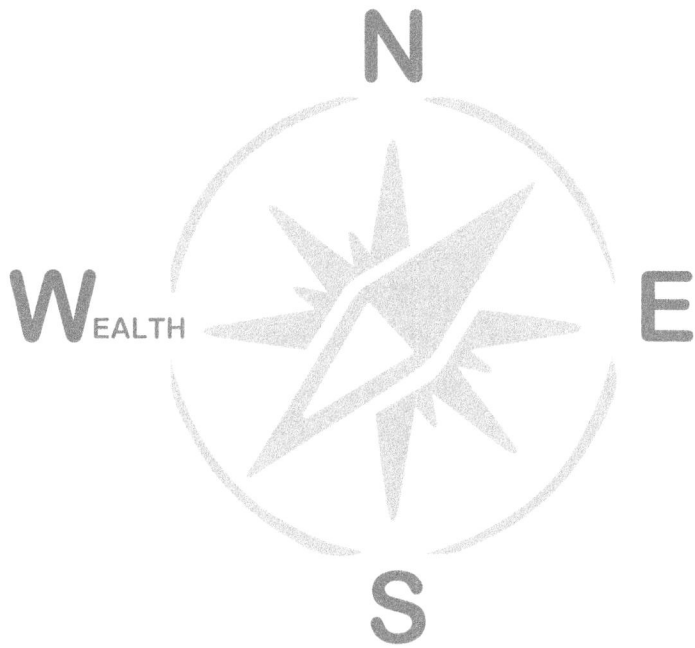

THE LIFE COMPASS

06
ACHIEVING WEALTH

I would like to believe that most people have the qualities to make them successful. And money management is one of them. I'm always fascinated by the story of billionaire Sir Li Ka-Shing, age 88, Hong Kong investor and philanthropist, listed on the Forbes list as Hong Kong's richest person. He currently has a net worth of $31.2 Billion. Sir Li Ka-Shing is one of the most influential tycoons in Asia with business interests in everything from ports, utilities and telecom to real estate and retail. He has a record 290,000 employees in more than 50 nations working for him. Despite his immense wealth, he has a reputation for being frugal and wears an inexpensive Seiko wristwatch. He is a school dropout who married a rich woman and yet his wealth is self-made. A

> *"Try not to become a man of success, but rather try to become a man of value. "* -- **Albert Einstein**

poor boy that started working full-time at age 14, his rags-to-riches story is legendary. That's so amazing!

I started working in my dad's business in primary school after school. I remember looking forward to the long lorry ride from my hometown in Pontian, Malaysia, to Singapore. It was an exhilarating journey and the ride of a lifetime! Dad trained me to issue invoices and cash receipts, and I felt so important to carry out this key task. I guess entrepreneurship runs in my blood, and I like creating value and creating wealth. As the middle child in my family, my father gave me more responsibilities than his first born son, and heaped great expectations on me. My gender did not play a part in the selection process of who is capable to run a business. Under my father's mentoring, I learned the ropes of running a business and grew up very fast to be a pillar that my family and siblings could lean on. I remember a particularly difficult time when the family business fell into troubled waters, and I had to sacrifice my further education to help support the family. I subsequently ventured into my own business at age 25 in the hope of creating wealth for the family. Looking back, I am amazed I continued for 30 years just to carry on the family legacy. I had lost count of the many times I wanted to quit. Every time the thought came, a picture of my dad's face would flash in front of my eyes and my eyes would become wet. I'd then dismiss the thought of simply throwing in the towel. I wanted to make dad proud of me. My dad is a big role model in my life. He taught me all about money management and accounting.

Cash flow is the life blood of any business. Money management is extremely important if you run a business. All business owners need to understand how money comes in and goes out of their business - if you ignore budgeting details and you run into losses, your venture might fail. There are many similarities between budgeting for yourself and budgeting for your business. When you understand the basics of money management for yourself, you will be more prepared to set up a budget for your company.

Similarly managing your money wisely is the best way to make sure you and your family gain financial security. To make it less overwhelming for you, here are some simple steps. First, start by setting financial goals and establishing a budget plan to help you achieve those goals. Financial goals are simply statements about things you wish you could afford. For example, you may have a goal to establish an emergency savings fund of three months of your salary, say $6,000 by the end of the year.

What are your personal financial goals? If you had $6,000, what would you do with it? Would you invest it in your small business? Would you put a down payment for

"Try not to become a man of success, but rather try to become a man of value. " **-- Albert Einstein**

your dream home? Would you buy a car? Would you spend it on a vacation? Would you save it in a US currency fixed deposit? Would you invest it in further education and pursue that degree to move up the corporate ladder?

You will be able to accomplish your goals if you manage your finances and put money aside on a regular basis. The key to success is to examine your Self (more of this in the next chapter), find out what it is that makes you jump out of bed each morning, and set SMART Financial Goals.

Specific, Measurable, Attainable, Realistic and Trackable
(SMART)

1. **Specific**. State exactly what you want to achieve, how you're going to do it and a timeline for when you want to achieve it. For example:

   Specific Goal Statement: *I want to pay off my credit card bill in 12 months by negotiating a payment plan with my bank.*

   General Goal Statement: *I want to improve my finances.*

2. **Measurable**. A financial goal should be measurable so you know when you have achieved it.

   Measurable Goal Statement: *In the next six months, I will get an in-principle approved bank loan and put a down payment for my dream property.*

   General Financial Goal Statement: *I will buy a property soon.*

3. **Attainable**. Make sure the financial goal is within reasonable reach.

   Attainable Goal Statement: *I will put aside $3 each day and save $1,000 in a year.*

   General Goal Statement: *I want to save money.*

"Try not to become a man of success, but rather try to become a man of value." **-- Albert Einstein**

4. **Realistic.** Is the financial goal realistic for you? Although you shouldn't ignore your limitations, your financial goals need to be tasks that you can reasonably accomplish.

    Realistic Goal Statement: *By managing my money well, next year I will be debt free and will have an emergency fund equal to three months of living expenses.*

    General Goal Statement: *By managing my money well, next year I will become a millionaire.*

5. **Trackable**. Being able to track your progress motivates you to keep going and reach your fiscal goal.

    Trackable Statement: *Each year I will save 10 percent more money than the previous year.*

    General Fiscal Goal Statement: *I will increase my savings goal every year.*

Get SMART about setting financial goals, and you will be well on your way to managing your money in a way that will provide financial security for you and your family for years to come. Society makes the mistake of equating wealth with tangible assets like the 5Cs. But money is not everything and you need to ask yourself if material wants will lead you to a fulfilling life. Would it be far better to invest in your intangible assets such as knowledge and education, social capital of networks, your worth, brand reputation and credibility? Actually money is only the means to an end and wealth is true happiness, good health and inner peace. Happiness is the by-product of Success. When you are truly happy, you've become a wealthy and successful person. There is no price tag on Happiness.

WORKING WITH NATURE LAWS

THE LIFE COMPASS

07
WORKING WITH NATURE LAWS

The key to live full satisfying lives is to simply dream up the things that we want to do and then make them happen! A simplistic statement to make but few people can actually put it into practice. Regardless of what you wish for, the best way to get it is to first have a clear mental picture of what you want in as much detail as possible. This can be hard work and few are willing to pay the entry fee for success.

Success takes dedication, planning, effort and giving up something to make it happen. It's the "half empty or half full glass" deal. If your life (your time) is already full to the top, there's no room for anything new. The entry fee

*"If you want to become successful in life, there is only one formula. Follow the Law of Nature." -- **Deep Trivedi***

is carving out the time to create that something new. Less recreational time, less time with the kids, less TV, less "me time". Paying the entry fee means going to work on your business or your book when the kids are asleep. And then there are excuses and lies that we tell ourselves. I need to go to college or university to have a successful career. There is an expectation that everyone needs to go to University. And even with a degree, you are not guaranteed to earn more money and be wildly successful. So is it a case of Nurture versus Nature?

One of my favorite role models is Sir Li Ka-Shing. Forced to drop out of school before the age of 15 due to his father's demise, the young Li found a job in a plastics trading company where he worked 16 hours a day. In 1950 he started his own company, Cheung Kong Industries. From manufacturing plastics, Li developed his company into a leading real estate investment company in Hong Kong that is public listed on the Hong Kong Stock Exchange since 1971. Now the richest person in Hong Kong and the second richest person in Asia, his companies make up 4% of the market capitalization of the Hong Kong Stock Exchange. Considered one of the most influential figures in Asia, Li was named "Asia's Most Powerful Man, Li Ka-Shing" by Asiaweek in 2001. Forbes Magazine and the Forbes family honored Li Ka-Shing with the first ever "Malcolm S. Forbes Lifetime Achievement Award" in 2006, in

Singapore. Here is a man who rose against the odds to carve out his own destiny, and did not allow his disadvantaged childhood to trip him up. He did not have a college education. He is a school dropout.

Don't get me wrong. I firmly believe that education is the ticket out of poverty. That is why I fought so hard to stay in school when my brother and parents wanted to stop my education in Form 2. They did not see the value of putting a girl through school and would prefer to give that privilege to their son. I begged them to let me stay in school and even put myself through night school to sit for my Cambridge "A" Levels whilst holding a full-time job in the day. In this way, I made sacrifices and completed my Pre-University education.

Like me, I'm sure you probably want to achieve your goal as fast as possible. I work with nature laws and get unhappy if placed in surroundings that are out of harmony. I know that it is so important to "tune in" and be in union with the Universe. I set my intention and surrender it to the Universe, then watch the magic happen. I focus on my goal daily. Consistent daily focus is absolutely necessary to "burn in" the new neural pathways I need to create my new goal. Without daily focus, the old mental habits that have kept you from attaining your goal will take over. The only way to override your subconscious mind that sabotage your success

> *"If you want to become successful in life, there is only one formula. Follow the Law of Nature."* -- **Deep Trivedi**

is to consciously focus on what you DO want, NOT what you DON'T want – and build new neural pathways! When you give energy to what you do want, you attract it and work with Nature laws. That's why success is an everyday event.

My belief is that when I am one with Nature and the Universe, I am in harmony and things will somehow fall into place for me. Then I get better at focusing on my goal. It will be the same for you.

Time and tide waits for no man. If you allow procrastination to exist in your life, you are giving it permission to delay your success. You deserve better. Make this a positive thought and your daily mantra. Re-commit to your goal every day. Don't let your goal take a back seat to the daily distractions of life. Life will try to get in your way. Just stay on course every day. Meditate on your goal daily. Focus on success!

Here are some practical steps you can take to be one with Nature laws.

1. Learn to listen to your body

Many of us have led busy lives for so long that we are out of touch with how we feel. Sometimes a situation will present itself and we will freak out and find that we have lost control. This actually results from a build-up of pent-up emotions that we are unaware of.

2. Accept responsibility for your feelings

No one can make you feel lousy. Rather you choose how you think and feel based on what you interpret the situation to be. Blaming others gives away your power and makes you fall into the victim mentality trap. You then react with anger and resentment.

"If you want to become successful in life, there is only one formula. Follow the Law of Nature." **-- Deep Trivedi**

3. **Talk to a trusted friend or counselor**

   Finding a safe space where you are able to express your feelings without being judged provides an opportunity to release pent-up emotions and allows you to feel at peace with yourself.

4. **Accept your imperfections**

   No one is perfect. You are not supposed to be perfect. Learning to accept yourself with all your strengths and weaknesses can give you peace within. Stop being your own inner critic. Thinking you have to be perfect and not being good enough is not going to get you anywhere. When feeling inadequate you judge yourself harshly and no matter what you do it will never be 'good enough'. Stop feeling like a loser and start making peace with yourself.

5. Let go of the past

The past is over and you did the best you could with what you knew at that time. If the past brings up memories of painful experiences for you, release the memories and heal the situation. Forgive others and yourself. This doesn't mean you condone these behaviors. It means you refuse to be held hostage by the memories and the old wounds to find your own inner peace and healing.

6. Learn to relax

There are many methods for staying in balance and harmony. Choose one that fits your lifestyle. Practicing meditation daily, yoga, reading, exercising, walking, or creating a sacred space where you can spend time to recharge and feel refreshed are all methods that take you away from focusing on 'what is wrong' to seeing yourself as being 'in control'.

"If you want to become successful in life, there is only one formula. Follow the Law of Nature." -- ***Deep Trivedi***

7. Keep a gratitude journal

Practice gratitude. What you pay attention to increases as you give energy to your thoughts. Thoughts of peace, love, success and abundance promotes inner healing and peace and leads to living lives that feel more balanced and harmonious.

Keep a journal. Journaling is a great tool to release emotions and make sense of what is going on in the world. This journal or notebook is for your eyes only and allows you to say anything you want without anybody seeing it except you. Once expressed, emotions tend to dissipate and you will find they are released through this practice. If this process doesn't totally release them the first time, repeat the exercise.

8. Spend time in nature

We are part of nature and when we re-connect with the natural world we touch our inner self and find a spiritual connection to something more. That something more is our connection to the Universal Energy whether we call it God, Source, All That Is, or Higher Power. Whatever we call it, when we feel connected to the 'Whole' we recognize our place in the world and feel a sense of peace and harmony and that 'all is right in our world.' That is being one with Nature and inviting harmony into our life.

EXAMINING MY SELF

THE LIFE COMPASS

08
EXAMINING MY SELF

Keeping your dream alive involves being honest and making a self-inventory list. It is customary for people to take stock and reflect on their achievements as each year ends, and look ahead to a brand new year. If you would like to start getting the benefits from examining the Self, then I have some thought provoking questions for you. These questions were developed for my Life Compass life coaching model that I have taught at many of my workshops.

Take out a piece of paper and pen. Then answer these questions as truthfully as you can. It may take a couple of hours for you to work through the list of questions, and the last question may involve some research. Take this to your

"Be not angry that you cannot make others as you wish them to be, since you cannot make yourself as you wish to be." —**Thomas Kempis**

mastermind group, run through with a trusted friend, or speak to your coach or mentor. Or even your competitor!

The 7 W and 1 H theory:

- Who am I now and why? (Diagnosing)

- Where am I heading to? (Goals)

- Why do I want to go there? (Justification)

- How can I reach there? (Planning)

- When will I reach there? (Time)

- What is the best way to get there? (Strategy)

- What it takes to win? (Key Success Factors)

- Who else are there? (Competition)

On top of this, a valuable resource is this book titled "Your Best Year Yet: Ten Questions for Making the Next Twelve Months Your Most Successful Ever" by Jinny S. Ditzler. I highly recommend it if you want to go a little deeper on examining the Self. These questions are designed to help you to bring the year to completion on a powerful note and to start the new year on a clean slate. I invite you to look at these following questions once a year, once a month or whenever you're looking for some direction in your life. If you want to be successful, you need to take a good hard look at your life and you will get a lot more out of it if you're more conscious about what you're creating.

Reflecting on this past year:

1. What do I want to be acknowledged for?
2. What did I accomplish?
3. What did I say I would do that I didn't do? (Do I still want to do this?)
4. What were my biggest disappointments?
5. What did I learn? – List three lessons which will make the most difference if you remember them this year.

Changing your paradigm:

1. How do I limit myself? How can I transform these actions to be powerful?
2. What do I say to myself to explain my failures? (These false beliefs are your limiting paradigm).
3. List your limiting paradigm.
4. List your new paradigm which must be personal, positive, present tense, powerfully and simply stated, pointing to an exciting future.
5. Read your new paradigm out loud when you are awake and before going to bed each day. Teach your

> *"Be not angry that you cannot make others as you wish them to be, since you cannot make yourself as you wish to be."* —***Thomas Kempis***

subconscious mind that this is your paradigm.

Looking ahead in the new year:

1. What are my personal values? What is most important to me in my life? What drives me?
2. Where is my life out of balance? If I could put one problem behind me, once and for all, what would it be?
3. What is my major focus for next year? (In what area do I want a breakthrough performance?)
4. What are my goals?

There is much power in committing to your goals by writing them down. The way this works is that you don't examine your Self only once a year. At least once a month or every 6 months, you ask yourself the above questions. Write them down and do it in writing several different times. Then after doing that for all of the above questions you answer one final question:

What do I want to accomplish and who do I want to be in the coming year?

To some, a five-year plan seems like an eternity. So a good way to revisit your goals every six months is to ask these questions. When you plan it this way, you give yourself the gift of self-reflection that will help you to create the life you really want this year. It only takes a little time to plan and some effort. Don't you deserve better than settling for whatever shows up when you fail to plan? "If you fail to plan, you plan to fail."

I worked with Eryan on his Life Compass and eventually worked the anger and resentment for his parents out of his system. And surprise! Eryan came around to even planning to enrol for a law degree. He is now taking steps to manifest that dream, much to the delight of his parents. This, I have listed as my breakthrough performance in the above questionnaire.

THINK BIG

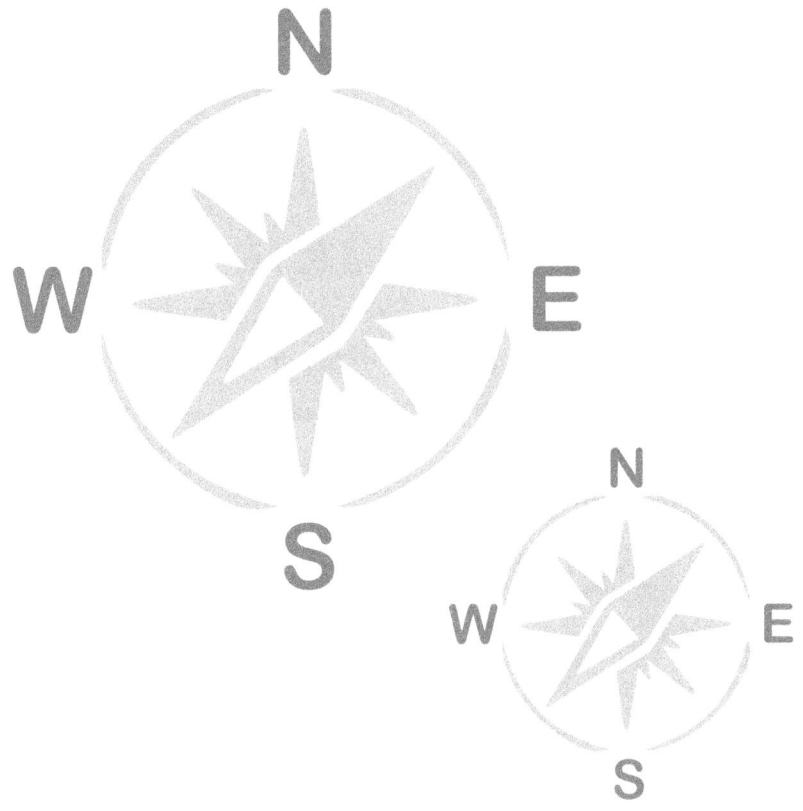

THE LIFE COMPASS

09
THINK BIG

If you want to be a leader, you have to think big. Big thoughts go hand in hand with big actions. Do them together and you can certainly make your dreams come true. This process is simple and direct, as you just need to apply the law of manifestation.

Think big and you will achieve great things in life. Look at the great men and the rich people around us. Think small and you will live small. With the courage to dream and think big, you are going to achieve a whole new level of results. Dream of a small house in life then that's what you are going to receive. Desire more and be willing to work to go after that, and you are going to get more.

> *"If you're going to be thinking anything, you might as well think big."*
> *-- Donald Trump*

Our brain is stimulated by emotions and feelings. Your feelings of "I want this very badly" will spur your commitment and determination to a level that would allow you to push past your limits and comfort zone to reach your goals. Search deep inside you to truly understand the reasons "Why" you need to reach those goals. Once you understand them, pen your goals down on paper to create an impression in your subconscious mind.

Then take BIG actions that correspond to your big thoughts! If you are searching for your dream house, see how much it costs and plan on how to manifest it into material form in your life. All of us want to be successful, but it depends on how badly we want it. There is a big difference between what we want and what we actually have. Today, I will give you clues whether what you are doing now in your life will lead you to a successful future or not. You will know without any doubt whether you are on the right track or you are moving towards a dead end future.

One of the secrets to Success is revealed by Michael Korda: "Your chance of success are directly proportional to the degree of pleasure you derive from what you do." Your success in life is measured by the degree of pleasure you are experiencing with what you are doing. If you love what you do, you are on the fast track to success. You can only really excel when you love what you do. You can't attain peak performance until you love what you do, and you will not have enough motivation to persist on your goals without loving what you do.

If you hate your life and hate what you do now, whatever it is, then you have very slim chances of success. You may say, "What can I do? I am in the wrong course that I hate but must finish?" Or "I have a job that I can't leave due to a lot of family commitments". I agree with all of that and will not tell you to go now and leave what you are doing whatever it is because you will not be successful in the end.

You must be on a path where you love what you do. And to do that you have to start now to define your life purpose. Besides thinking big, defining your life purpose is the first step towards leading a fulfilling and successful life. You have to know the path that will let you live with passion and make a difference to other people's lives. When you discover your life purpose you will have the power of Choice and to make changes until you are aligned with the right direction; the direction of your life purpose and your ultimate destiny.

It is not possible to change your path overnight. But it pays to start now to do the necessary preparation and soon, with cumulative small changes, you will be on the right track. Don't you agree with me that you will only succeed when you

> *"If you're going to be thinking anything, you might as well think big."*
> *-- **Donald Trump***

do what you love? And what if you fail?

Perhaps regarded as one of the greatest United States presidents of all time, Abraham Lincoln's early life might not have reflected his potential greatness. He failed in business. He lost election to the state legislature, Speaker of the House, nomination for Congress, appointment of land officer, U.S. Senate twice and nomination for Vice President. But he did not quit. He continued to dream big. After those eight huge failures, Lincoln was elected President of the United States. How many of us would have persevered like Lincoln did?

Many problems that we think of today pale in comparison to what happened in the late 1850's and middle 1860's during Lincoln's presidency. There were several key challenges that Lincoln faced as U.S. President. Lincoln was President during the American Civil War, which lasted four years. About five weeks after Lincoln was inaugurated as the 16th United States President, the American Civil War began. Lincoln was President of a country that was literally falling apart.

Division may exist between families. Some families were divided so much by the war that one son may have fought for the North while another son of the same family fought for the South. During the Lincoln Administration, 600,000 to 700,000 Americans perished in the Civil War – a record high. The American Civil War casualties exceed the United States'

| 61

losses in all of its other wars from The American Revolution to the present.

Do any of us think that we have such an enormous responsibility? Lincoln had an unbearable responsibility of having the most American casualties during his term as President. More Americans died from war during Lincoln's presidency than all of the other American Presidents combined.

Lincoln fell into depression and did not have access to antidepressants, such as Prozac, to take as prescription medication. He never had the luxury of having access to modern treatments. Lincoln's job was to deal with a country that was divided by war. At times, your problems may seem as huge as Lincoln's struggles, mainly because you are the one who is currently enduring a particular problem. All of us have common and unique problems. Can you imagine if you weren't so lucky and had limited access to treatments like Lincoln? Fortunately, we do have the luxury of modern medicine and modern hospitals.

On April 9, 1865, Lincoln was assassinated five days after the Civil War ended and died the morning after he was shot. This was the thanks that he got after he united his country as President, issued the Emancipation Proclamation to end slavery, inspired numerous people while suffering from

> *"If you're going to be thinking anything, you might as well think big."*
> *-- Donald Trump*

depression and was one of the most memorable Presidents America has ever had?

Do you still want to complain about how you feel unappreciated for the work you've done? Lincoln moved mountains and he was killed. He never lived to see the results of what he implemented. The United States owes Lincoln a huge debt of gratitude.

Like Lincoln, every one of us has overcome problems and has achieved greatness in our own way. You had to overcome obstacles to learn to walk or talk. There are challenges you overcame that you probably do remember very well, such as finishing a project, winning a contest, graduating from school or establishing a career. Every one of you has a potential for greatness like Abraham Lincoln. It is up to you to find the greatness within yourself.

In addition, a New York Times article ("Personal Health" by Jane E. Brody; March 27, 2017) says a positive outlook may be good for your health and longevity. To quote from the article:

"'Look on the sunny side of life."

"Turn your face toward the sun, and the shadows will fall behind you."

"Every day may not be good, but there is something good in every day."

"See the glass as half-full, not half-empty."

Researchers are finding that thoughts like these, the hallmarks of people sometimes called "cock eyed optimists," can do far more than raise one's spirits. They may actually improve health and extend life. There is no longer any doubt that what happens in the brain influences what happens in the body. When facing a health crisis, actively cultivating positive emotions can boost the immune system and counter depression. Studies have shown an indisputable link between having a positive outlook and health benefits..."

So set the stage for happiness and hope, surround yourself with positive minded people, do good, keep a gratitude journal, and think positive thoughts. Think BIG.

SOS, EOE, NON, WOW

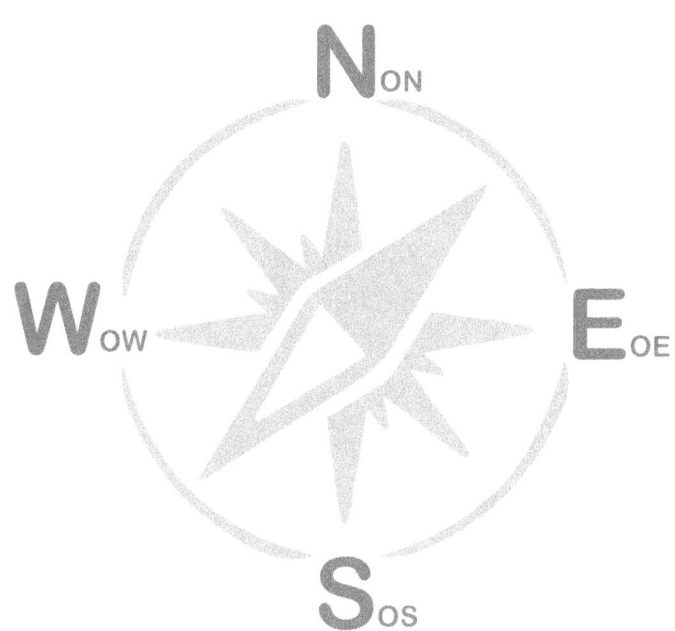

THE LIFE COMPASS

10

SOS, EOE, NON, WOW

In the fascinating life of the iconic South African leader and Nobel Peace Prize Winner Nelson Mandela (1918 – 2013), it was **Think DIFFERENT**. Expelled from University for joining a student protest, Nelson Mandela was in and out of jail. In 1952, at ANC (African National Congress) as President of the Youth League in his Defiance Campaign against apartheid laws, Mandela and 19 others were charged for treason and sentenced to nine months imprisonment. He completed his studies in prison and graduated with an LLB degree through Unisa 27 years later.

"If you are always trying to be normal, you will never know how amazing you can be!"
— *Maya Angelou*

First arrested on August 5 1962, charged with leaving the country illegally and encouraging the strike, Mandela was sentenced to five years in prison. While serving his sentence, the police connected him with more serious crimes of treason and sabotage. He was sentenced to life imprisonment in June 1964 with seven others. His mother and his eldest son passed away while Mandela was in prison and sadly, he was prohibited to attend their funerals.

Mandela was sent to Robben Island, off the coast of Cape Town, where he endured 18 years of hard labor. He was not allowed contact with the outside world and only had a few visitors. In 1988 he was taken to hospital to be treated for tuberculosis. Three months later he was moved to Victor Verster Prison where he spent his last 14 months in prison. He was released on Sunday, February 11 1990, nine days after the unbanning of the ANC, and after 27 years in prison – thin and grey. Other political prisoners were also freed and exiles returned. The ANC began talking to the government about South Africa's future. For this work he and President FW de Klerk won the Nobel Peace Prize in 1993, and in April 1994, Mandela ran for South Africa's first democratic elections.

On May 10 1994, Mandela was inaugurated as South Africa's first democratically elected President and served one term of office. In his retirement he continued serving the people. He worked on building schools and clinics, highlighting HIV, children and leadership. He died at his home in Johannesburg on December 5 2013 and the world mourned the loss of a great leader.

"I learned that courage was not the absence of fear, but the triumph over it. The brave man is not who he does not feel afraid, but he who conquers fear."- **Nelson Mandela.**

Great leadership is the key to success. Great communication is the key to great leadership. Think of any great leader in modern times: Gandhi, Martin Luther King, Jr, Nelson Mandela and John F. Kennedy come to mind immediately. They were powerful leaders because they could inspire and lead people. They were able to articulate their vision and that made them so successful in achieving their goals.

"If you are always trying to be normal, you will never know how amazing you can be!"
— *Maya Angelou*

My secret formula is **SOS**. SOS is an acronym for Serve Our Soul. It is also important to be in alignment with your Life Compass. The Life Compass serves these purposes:

1. To be a man of high ethical standards.
2. To build a harmonious environment.
3. To unify Man and Nature.
4. To have adequate living and a blissful life.

Our Values

You best serve yourself by your values. Make sure your values – both personal and professional – tie in with your team. You must clearly know your personal values and your organization values to lead effectively. For example, answer these questions as honestly as you can.

Personally:

1. What do you stand for?
2. What is most important to you?
3. What is your personal mission in life?

Professionally:

1. What do you stand for?
2. What are you willing to do to get new business?
3. What are you not willing to do?
4. Do you have a professional mission statement?

In "The Doctrine of the Mean" By Zi Si (Confucius's grandson) written 500 B.C.E (both a doctrine of Confucianism and also the title of one of the Four Books of Confucian philosophy), this is seen as Self-Cultivation. Self-Cultivation is fundamental to the study of Confucianism. "If the fundamental is chaotic, the branches will not achieve order. With self-cultivation, Dao (virtues) will be established."

So by your ready answers to the questions above, you are establishing order in your mind. The purpose of study is to observe and endeavor knowledge (do one's best to pursue knowledge).

Confucius also said leaders must show sincerity of intention:

"Therefore, a man of noble character is discreet when he is alone. His words give consideration to his deeds, his deeds give consideration to his words, his words match with his deeds. A man with noble character must have sincere intention."

Leaders don't change their values over time or to achieve short-term success. Their words match their deeds. Values are the house rules by which you play the game. A well-defined value system makes all decision-making easier and encourages your team to go where you lead.

"If you are always trying to be normal, you will never know how amazing you can be!"
― *Maya Angelou*

Our Vision

It's easy to say you have a vision for your business and organization. It's on your notice board. You know it inside out. Sharing it widely with your team is important too. Even more importantly, your vision for the business must provide a unifying picture so that everyone on the team – from the manager to the tea lady - can see exactly where you're going and the importance of their role in getting there. Therefore, the clearer the concept and the clearer the message is, the more likely you and your team can achieve the goal. KISS (Keep It Simple Silly) is a good way to go for Vision Statement. Make sure your Vision is 100% participative and inclusive. It can't be a top-down decision.

Our Environment (EOE)

You know you are serving your higher soul purpose when you are on the right track and attracting success. And one way of service is to be a good and great leader. Andrew Carnegie said: "You must capture and keep the heart of the original and supremely able man before his brain can do its best." When you understand what lies at the core of your team members, you can serve them and allow them to reach their full potential. Value their uniqueness. Your team members are your internal customers and stakeholders in the business. You must treat them at least as well as your external customers. This is the highest level of customer service.

Confucianism also teaches, "If we show consideration for the various officials, their reward and contribution will be significant." "If we are kind and take care of people, the people will be encouraged." "If we cherish the various dukes and princes, they will have fear with respect towards us."

Shape the right work environment and you'll have loyal team members following you. That means, you have to create a work environment that respects each person, appreciates them and rewards their effort big or small, and encourages an openness to change. Make it a safe environment, one which encourages innovation and creativity. When you harmonize and make each team member feel at home, they will feel they have a stake in the outcome. It will be an environment that promotes growth at all levels. Combine all these elements and you have a winning formula for inspiring greatness and leading to breakthrough success.

Who says you cannot create the life you desire? When you are able to delete negativity from your conscious mind, accept responsibility, think positive thoughts and want success very badly, it can happen. According to the Doctrine of the Mean, it is also important to balance one's mood. That is, to keep the mood balanced and be optimistic.

"If you are always trying to be normal, you will never know how amazing you can be!"
— *Maya Angelou*

Therefore it's important to control mood swings or energy shifts if you want to maintain your balance and be successful in life and business. According to psychologist and researcher Martin Seligman, some people appear to be wired to respond in an optimistic manner to work life balance upset and life's ups and downs. Others are wired for opposite responses. Fortunately, you do not have to settle for the wiring you were born with. With practice you can improve your resilience and your hopefulness by acquiring positive thinking skills.

I liken it to building your physical fitness regime: it takes attention, concentration, commitment, and a routine. If you approach a workout program with those qualities, you can almost always improve your fitness.

Remember SOS. Don't wait until you need it as a lifeline. Take the first step and use my Life Compass to chart your journey for success. Here are Four Easy Steps to attain your goal:

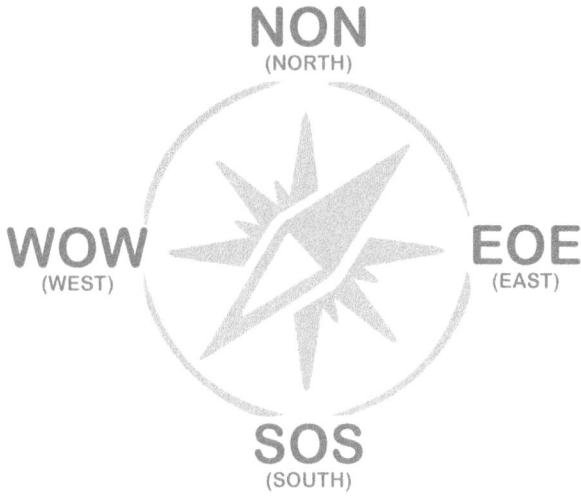

N is for NON (Now or Never)

- Time and tide wait for no man. Do it now and do it well.

S is for SOS (Serve Our Soul)

- Ask our inner self what we really want. Let the soul lead us to a more fulfilling life.

E is for EOE (Explore Our Environment)

- Explore the people, work, the things we surround ourselves with, in order to find balance and harmony.

W is for WOW (World of Wisdom)

- Come from a space of abundance. Wisdom will lead us to a peaceful and fruitful life.

"If you are always trying to be normal, you will never know how amazing you can be!"
— ***Maya Angelou***

The Life Compass is a useful tool to navigate life's twists and turns and make you a winner. It has helped my charges like Eryan go from a wounded place to one of wholesomeness and reconciliation with his parents. It has guided my friends to live out their dream and not kill it in its infancy. It has made life WOW and good again. A good life is one when you assume nothing, do more, need less, laugh a lot, smile often, dream big and be in eternal gratitude for how blessed you are. When you consult the Life Compass as a purpose-driven conscious individual, you seek out knowledge and high ethical standards, pay attention to build a balanced harmonious environment, be in union with Nature/Universe and realize you don't need much for adequate living and a blessed life.

You must be thankful for the good and bad things in life that happen to you. The bad things for they open your eyes to the good things you weren't paying attention to before. Then you'd realize you are not lost and afraid anymore, like Eryan. You too can make a difference.

Henny In Action

Henny In Action

Henny In Action

www.ingramcontent.com/pod-product-compliance
Lightning Source LLC
Chambersburg PA
CBHW070307230526
45470CB00002B/768